HOBBY TIME
ADVENTURE JOURNAL

Creative Story Writing & Coloring Book

Make Your OWN Comics, Calendars & Mine Craft Art

By: Tolik Trishkin

The Thinking Tree Publishing Company, LLC

Just For Fun

JOURNAL

NAME & DATE:

CONTENTS:

Page 4 - Creative Story Writing, Drawing & Coloring Time

Page 118 - Make Your OWN Comics

Page 138 - Design Your OWN Calendars

Page 150 - Complete the Drawings

Pages 162 - Design your own Mine Craft Art

WWW.FUNSCHOOLINGBOOKS.COM

Designed By Sarah Janisse Brown

CREATIVE STORY WRITING, DRAWING AND COLORING TIME

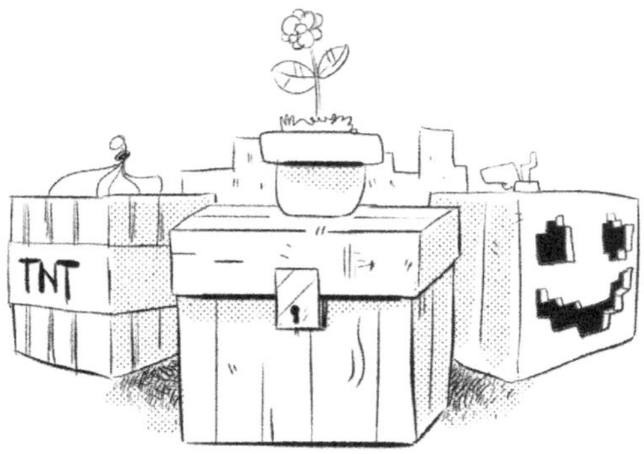
TNT

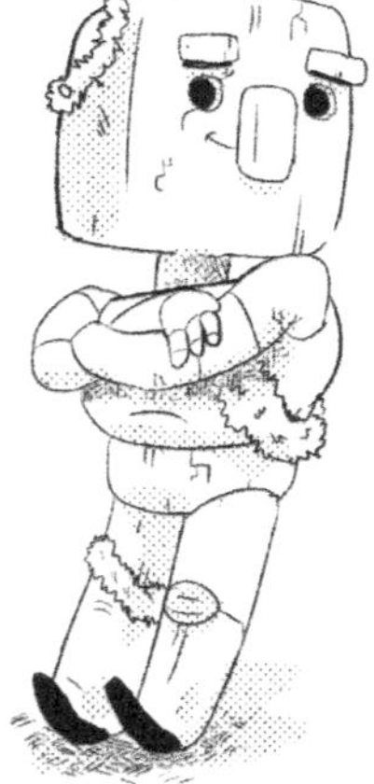

12345

TNT

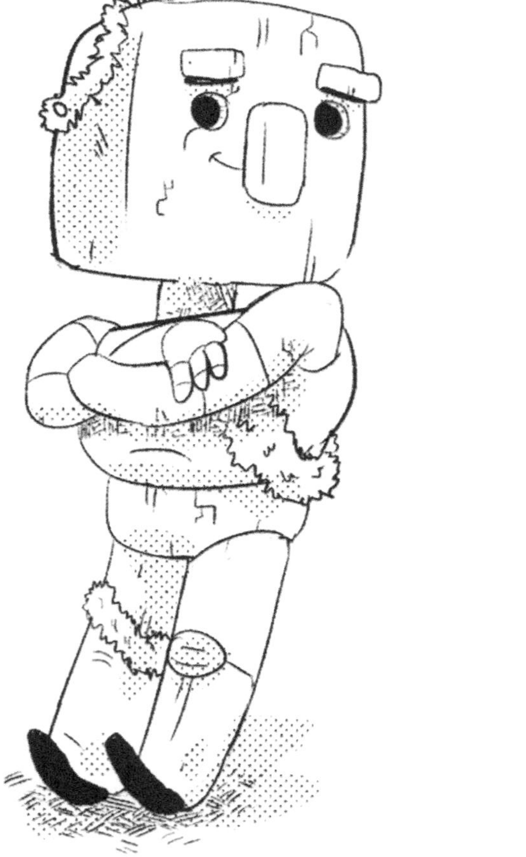

04

08091998

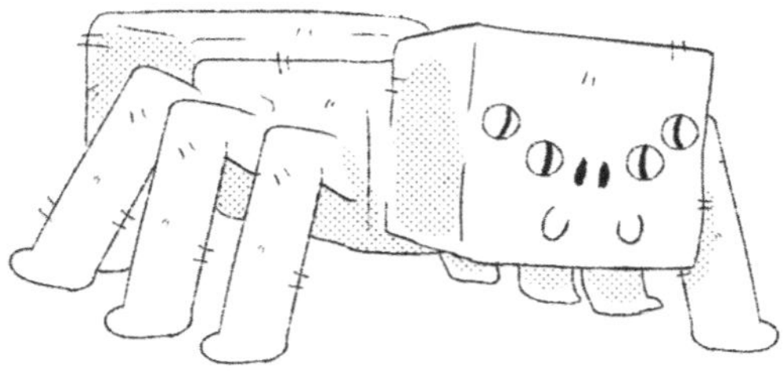

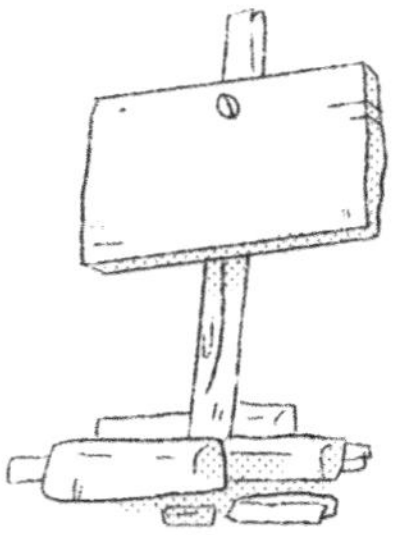

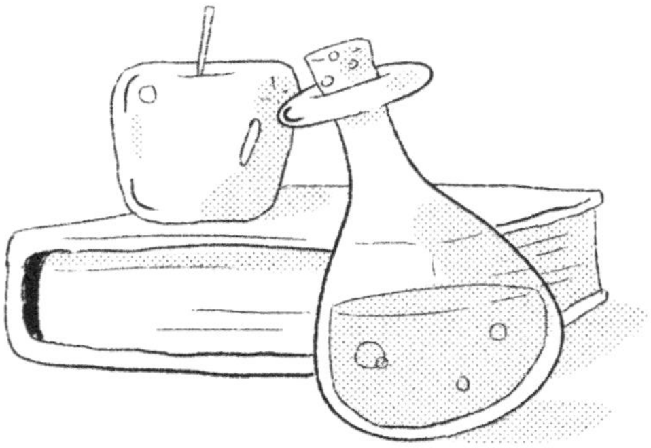

DRAW A PICTURE AND WRITE YOUR OWN STORY

CREATE YOUR OWN COMICS

CREATE YOUR OWN CALENDARS

Sunday	Monday	Tuesday	Wednesday	Thursday	Friday	Saturday

Sunday	Monday	Tuesday	Wednesday	Thursday	Friday	Saturday

Sunday	Monday	Tuesday	Wednesday	Thursday	Friday	Saturday

Sunday	Monday	Tuesday	Wednesday	Thursday	Friday	Saturday

Sunday	Monday	Tuesday	Wednesday	Thursday	Friday	Saturday

Sunday	Monday	Tuesday	Wednesday	Thursday	Friday	Saturday

Sunday	Monday	Tuesday	Wednesday	Thursday	Friday	Saturday

Sunday	Monday	Tuesday	Wednesday	Thursday	Friday	Saturday

Sunday	Monday	Tuesday	Wednesday	Thursday	Friday	Saturday

Sunday	Monday	Tuesday	Wednesday	Thursday	Friday	Saturday

Sunday	Monday	Tuesday	Wednesday	Thursday	Friday	Saturday

Sunday	Monday	Tuesday	Wednesday	Thursday	Friday	Saturday

COMPLETE THE DRAWING AND ADD COLOR!

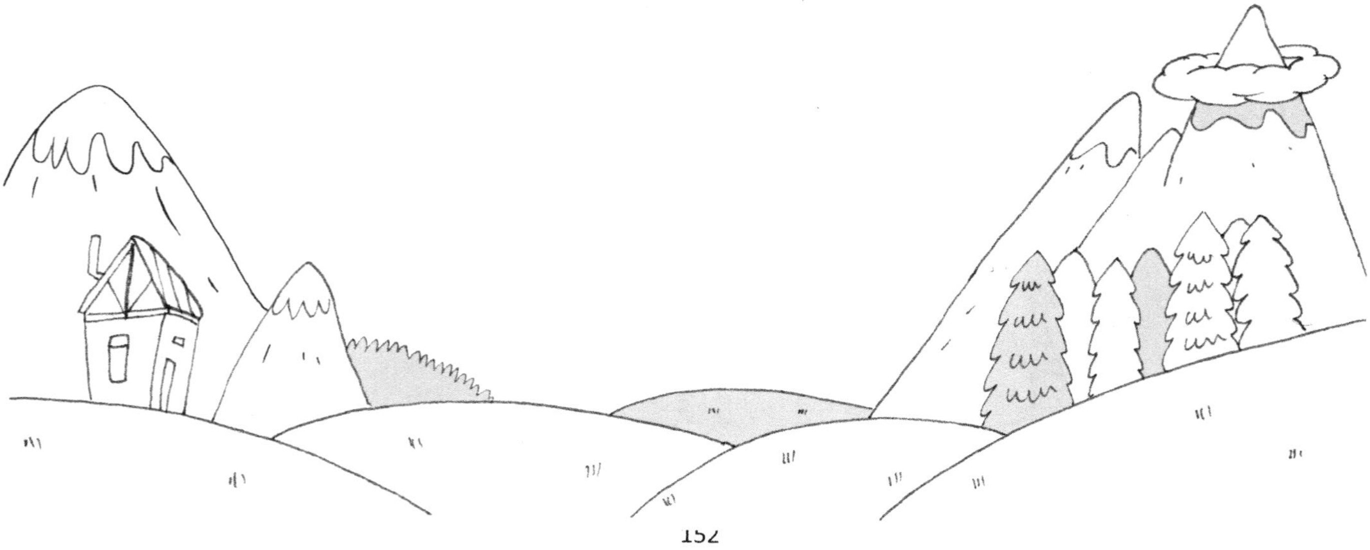

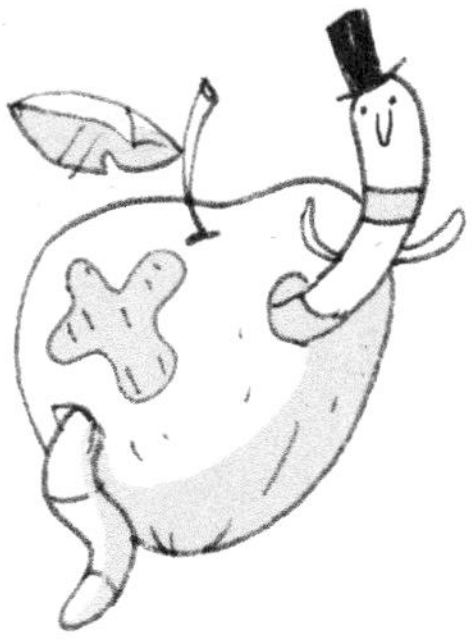
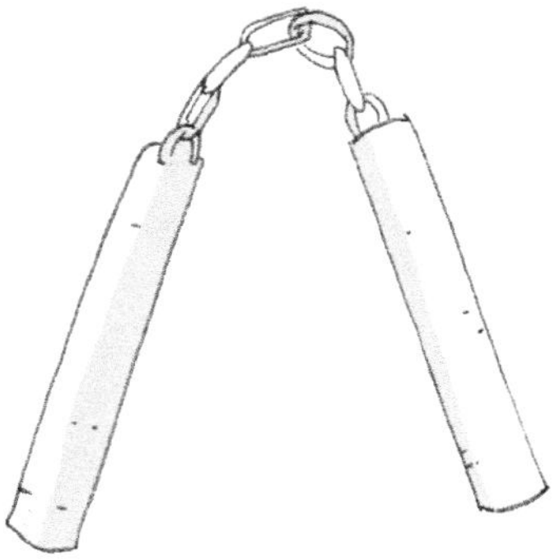
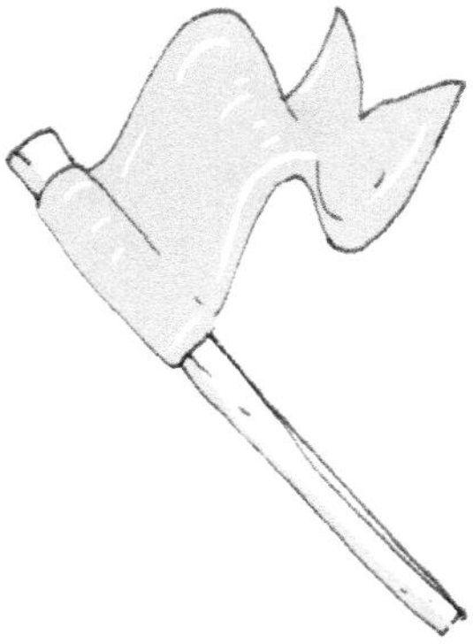

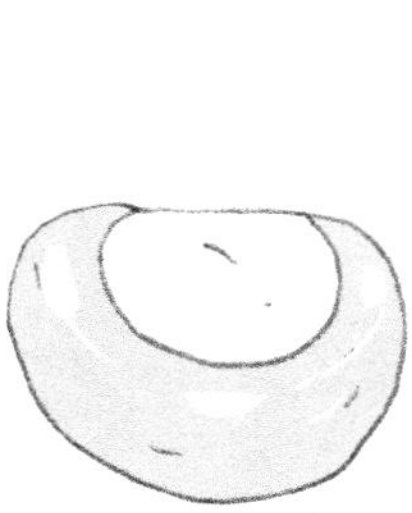
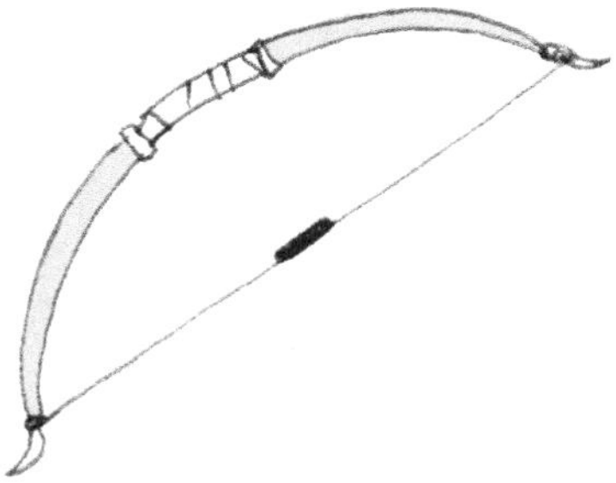
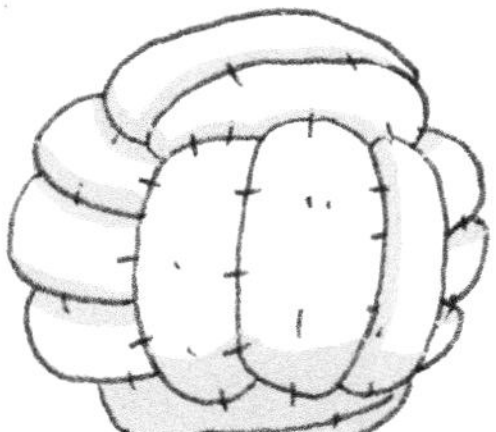

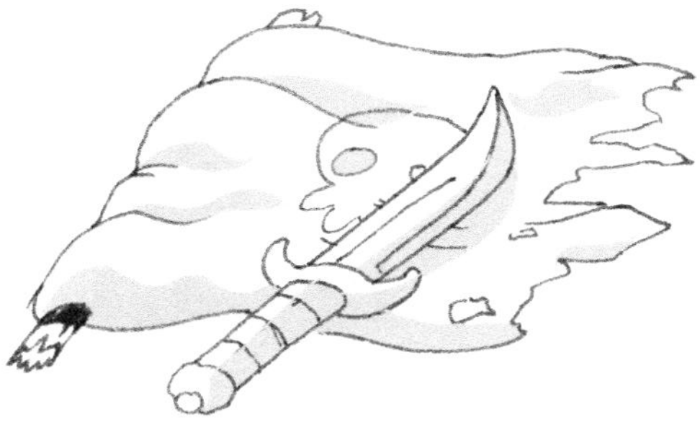

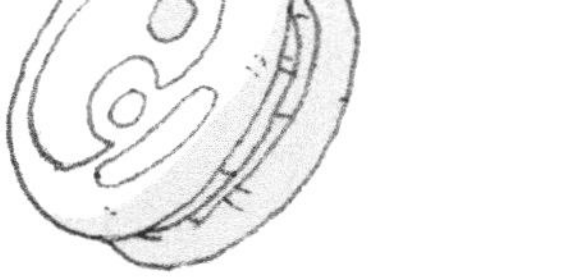
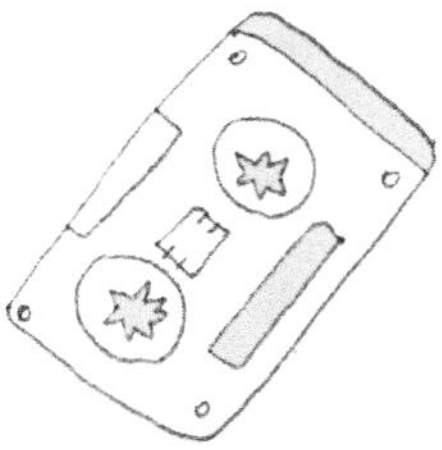
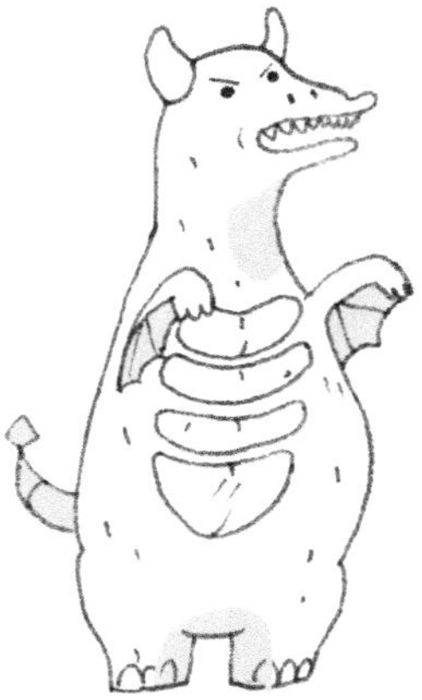
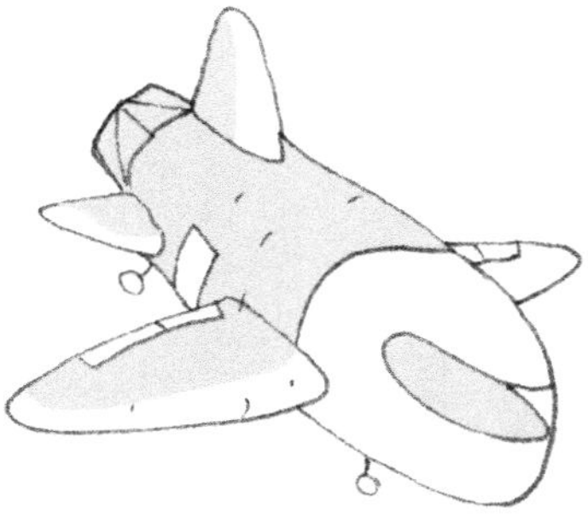
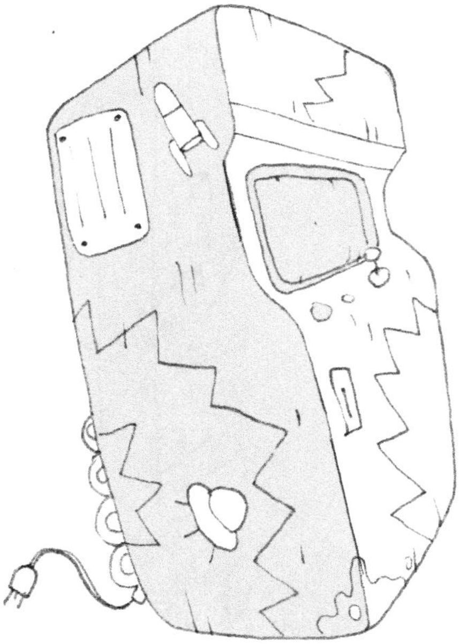
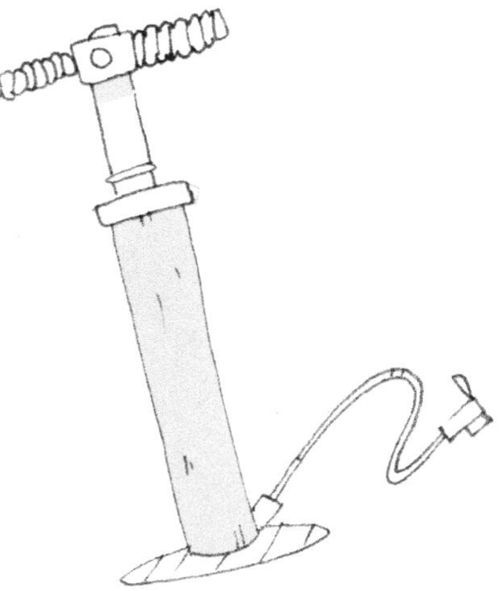

12345

MAKE YOUR OWN MINECRAFT ART AND DESIGNS

MAKE YOUR OWN MINE CRAFT ART & DESIGNS

MAKE YOUR OWN MINE CRAFT ART & DESIGNS

MAKE YOUR OWN MINE CRAFT ART & DESIGNS

MAKE YOUR OWN MINE CRAFT ART & DESIGNS

"SAY ANYTHING!"
"TRY NEW FONTS!"

Made in the USA
Middletown, DE
19 September 2024

61186871R00104